Fear

"God, why am I so afraid?"

By Donna Streufert
Edited by Jane L. Fryar

CPH

ST. LOUIS

Editorial assistant: Marilyn T. Weber

This publication is also available in braille and in large print for the visually impaired. Write to the Library for the Blind, 1333 South Kirkwood Road, St. Louis, MO 63122—7295. Allow six months for processing.

1 2 3 4 5 6 7 8 9 10 02   01 00 99 98 97 96 95 94 93

By mutual agreement . . .
and in the Holy Spirit's power

We will attend each session unless an

      emergency prevents our attendance.

We will listen to each other and show one another

      Christ-like love and concern.

We will contribute to the discussion in positive ways

      as we are able to do that.

We will rely on the Holy Scriptures as our final authority,

      knowing that human ideas and opinions,

      even the ideas and opinions of God's people, will

      likely stray from God's truth from time to time.

We will keep everything we hear confidential,

      sharing it with no one unless doing so

      is a matter (literally) of life and death.

We will use what we learn in this group to contribute

      even more fully to the overall ministry of

_____

      (*Put your congregation's name here.*)

We will respect one another's schedules by

      beginning and ending on time.

Contents

How to Use This Course   7

1. God, I'm Afraid—Why?   15

2. God, I'm Afraid—Jesus Responds
   to My Fear   25

3. God, I'm Afraid—Love Crowds Out Fear   35

4. God, I'm Afraid—Living in Faith,
   Growing in Trust   42

Helps for the Leader   49

Session 1   50

Session 2   53

Session 3   57

Session 4   61

How to Use This Course

Three ingredients will make it possible for you to maximize the usefulness of this course.

❖ 1—Prayer

Only as God invades our lives and touches our hearts can we grow up in Him. Ask and keep on asking for the Holy Spirit's direction and help as you approach His Word. Even if you work through the questions in this study on your own (and perhaps especially then), you must rely on God to do His work in you, His holy work of drawing you to Himself. He's the only one who can connect us to Himself and keep that connection strong. He's the only one who can connect us to our brothers and sisters in the faith and keep those connections strong. We need to ask Him to do that.

❖ 2—Care

That is, care for one another in your group. Dietrich Bonhoeffer once wrote, "Christianity means community through Jesus Christ and in Jesus Christ . . . we belong to one another only through and in Jesus Christ."

Only God can create the kind of care, the kind of community, the kind of connectedness that we see modeled by the early Christian church. It's His gift to His people. We can't make it happen, no matter how slick our techniques, no matter how smooth our approach.

But we can, by God's grace, encourage the kind of atmosphere, the kind of love and acceptance, in which His people

❖

come to know one another as brothers and sisters in the faith and not as third or fourth cousins.

❖ 3—As We Share

How does that kind of love happen? We cannot drum it up by our own effort, no matter how up-to-date our methodology. Neither can we force any believer or group of believers to talk about their faith with one another, to share their needs and hurts with each other, or to admonish and console one another. We can, however, use what we know about human relationships to create a safe haven, an island of time and place, in which God's people can relax, get to know one another, and, eventually, feel free to let down their guard.

In this kind of setting, participants can experience the freedom to talk about their hurts and their faith with each other, if they choose to do that. They can encourage one another in the one true faith, just as the early Christians did and as the holy apostles also urge us to do as God's chosen people today (1 Thessalonians 4:18; 5:11).

❖ On to the Practical

As you develop small-group ministry in your congregation, you need to keep an overarching vision in mind. But to get small-group Bible study off the ground, and to keep it functioning effectively, you also need to think through some practical considerations.

Leadership

Talk with your pastor about this. He has both the right and the duty to oversee any Bible-study program in your congregation. He himself may lead some groups. And he may decide to delegate some leadership tasks, approving those who will teach and taking care to see that they receive adequate training.

In general, all those who lead small-group Bible studies will be people who

- demonstrate an understanding of Law and Gospel, sin and grace, not just intellectually, but in their relationships with God and with other people;
- demonstrate an ability to communicate the truths of the Scriptures clearly;
- express a desire to be used by God to disciple others;
- show a commitment to the entire congregation and submission to the authority of the pastor, not competing with other leaders or programs;
- know or be willing to learn techniques that enable adults to examine and apply their faith to their daily lives;
- pray for the group and the congregation regularly;
- have time to plan, prepare, and lead a small-group Bible study on an ongoing, consistent basis;
- demonstrate the emotional and spiritual maturity to accept responsibilities of leadership, to receive direction and sometimes criticism with wisdom and grace, to share personal strengths and weaknesses with appropriate vulnerability, and to respond to others with Christlike humility and love.

Setting

Many people find a home conducive to the relaxed, casual atmosphere you want to foster. In any case, you will need a meeting place where

- from 6–10 people can sit comfortably and see one another as they converse;
- the chairs are comfortable;
- the room is suitably lighted, ventilated, and at a comfortable temperature;
- coffee, tea, or soft drinks and an occasional snack can be served without danger of damaging carpets or upholstery;

- children can be adequately supervised while they play away from the Bible-study group.

Supplies

Everyone who attends should bring his or her own Bible. In addition you will need
- copies of this Study Guide for everyone (note the leader's materials in the back of this guide);
- pens or pencils, one for everyone;
- songbooks, hymnals, and perhaps an instrument to accompany singing during worship times;
- an empty chair or two placed prominently to remind everyone of the opportunity to invite guests—in particular, unchurched friends or relatives.

❖ That First Meeting

The first time you're together, you will want to spend some time getting to know one another and establishing rules for the group.
- Introduce yourselves to one another. Do this even if only one person is unfamiliar to the others. Tell your name. Tell a little about your family. And tell how you've come to be in the group. Use a timer and allow each person to speak for about one minute.
- Agree on ground rules about questions like these:
    Who will bring snacks? How often?
    Will we provide childcare? If so, how? Will we take turns, hire someone and agree to all chip in to pay for it? Or?
    Will we meet in one location? Take turns hosting the group? Or?
    When will we begin? End? (Include dates and also times.)
- Read the "By Mutual Agreement" statement on page 3 of this guide. Talk it over until everyone understands it and

you truly have reached mutual agreement. Promise to reread this agreement as you begin each session, at least the first several times you get together.

- Talk about participation. This study asks group members to work with partners or with three or four other people. Agree to listen to one another with respect. Also agree to allow one another the freedom to "pass" on any question for any reason without having to state that reason.
- Remind one another that everyone is entitled to an opinion. However, in this group all human opinions must take a back seat to the Holy Scriptures. You will share lots of thoughts and feelings with one another during the next few weeks. At least you will, if this course is written well, and your leader(s) encourage participation as they should. Even so, we believe that absolute truth exists and that it can be known because the God who created the universe has revealed the truth for us in His Word. We bow to His wisdom. We submit to His truth.

❖ Elements of Small-Group Bible Studies

Most groups spend 60–90 minutes together in these four activities:
- Worship
- Bible study
- Prayer
- Fellowship

Worship (5–15 minutes)

As most small-group Bible studies begin, participants spend a few minutes in worship. Often this includes singing, especially if someone in the group can play the guitar or piano. If the group does not include a musician, someone in the group can usually find an alternative that will allow everyone to join in singing two or three hymns or songs. Some groups find that they manage to sing quite well a cappella. Some use prerecorded accompaniment tracks from cassette tapes or CDs.

Keep in mind, though, that worship involves much more than simply singing a few random songs. Worship should help participants quiet their hearts as the Lord prepares them to hear what He will to say to them in His Word.

Therefore, opening worship will almost always include a prayer for His peace and for hearts ready to receive His truth.

Bible Study (40–60 minutes)

Our relationship with our Lord deepens as we immerse ourselves in His Word. In that Word He confronts us with our sin and then comforts us with His forgiving love in our Savior. Small-group Bible study at its best provides for both of those processes to take place.

Materials appropriate for small-group study avoid a lecture format. Rather, they involve a mix of individual thought and writing, one-on-one discussions, and give-and-take conversations by the whole group. The leader facilitates, asks questions, provides nuggets of insight to push the group's process forward, and prays for participants while they think and talk with one another.

Prayer—(5–10 minutes)

In the small-group Bible study process, God's Word touches the hearts of His people. It probes pockets of hurt and sometimes of hardness. God's people talk with one another about life's most important issues. We think and laugh together. We question and cry together. It's only natural that we pray together too. It's not only natural, but necessary.

This kind of prayer models itself after that of the early church:

Committed by God's grace, to one another, and to the truth of His Word, God's people asked their Lord to intervene in their lives. Together they asked for His specific help with specific challenges and needs. They united their hearts in praise to Him for all He had done and for all that He had promised yet to do. They received from Him the power they needed to live as His witnesses in a world that is, even now for the most part, hostile to the claims Christ. We join them in the same kind of prayer.

Fellowship (10–20 minutes)

Christian fellowship means so much more than this spring's softball league or last Friday's fish fry. Of course, there is nothing wrong with playing softball or sharing a meal with other believers. But God intends that Christian fellowship (*koinonia*) cut more deeply below life's surface than that.

As we said earlier, only God can create genuine fellowship. It's His gift to His people. We can, however, provide unstructured time over coffee or lemonade before and after the more formal group time. This will free participants to laugh together, to cry together, to ask one another about ongoing personal and family concerns and simply to enjoy one another as members of God's family.

We witness spontaneously to one another about what God has done for us in Christ's cross and, then too, about what He is doing for us in our day-to-day lives. We have the chance to share specific prayer requests one-on-one and to become aware of needs God would use us to meet for each

❖

other. In short, we have a chance to be the church, the family of God, for one another.

❖ As You Begin This Course

What's This Course About?

In an episode of the TV series, "M*A*S*H," Col. Potter encounters a sentry while on his way to his office in the middle of the night. The sentry stops the colonel—but forgets to ask for the password.

During the conversation that follows, Col. Potter says, "You're trembling, son. Are you afraid?"

"No, Sir, just cold," the soldier replies.

To which Col. Potter responds, "If you were smart, you'd be afraid."

Fear floods every human heart at one time or another. The issue is not *if* we will experience it but *when,* and more important still, what will we do with fear when it strikes.

This course addresses those questions from the perspective of those who have heard the Son of God Himself say, "Don't be afraid, only believe." It encourages participants to ask the hard questions that arise when we're afraid. It urges participants to think about strategies for handling fear now— before they find themselves in the smoke and mud of life's fear-provoking battles. And it points the way to the arms of a Savior who wants to comfort and protect us no matter what dangers and worries we face now or may encounter in the future.

May that Savior hold you close to Himself as you explore what He has taught us about facing fear.

God, I'm Afraid— Why?

Setting Our Sights

In this session we will consider what causes us to feel afraid. We will review reasons the Scriptures suggest for our fear. We will explore our responses to fear and discover what to do when fear strikes.

Getting Started

Almost everyone endures nightmares occasionally. Recall one of yours. It need not be your worst or your most frightening—just one you recall. If you can do so comfortably, talk with a partner about your nightmare. What about it frightened you?

Digging In

Nightmares come from deep inside. They reflect our fears. Since all of us—occasionally at least—experience them, nightmares also evidence the fact that fear is universal among human beings. Some people deny their fears. They see fear as a sign of weakness. Nevertheless, fear is common to us all. It may attack us from any of three directions.

Fear: Source 1

We can become afraid when something

threatens our security, our physical well-being. We feel afraid when we sense "something bad might happen," when we face change, or loss.

> Then He [Jesus] got into the boat and His disciples followed Him. Without warning, a furious storm came up on the lake, so that the waves swept over the boat. But Jesus was sleeping. The disciples went and woke Him, saying, "Lord, save us! We're going to drown!"
>
> He replied, "You of little faith, why are you so afraid?" Then He got up and rebuked the winds and the waves, and it was completely calm.
>
> The men were amazed and asked, "What kind of man is this? Even the winds and the waves obey Him!" (Matthew 8:23–27).

1. How might the disciples have described their experience to their families when they returned home? What might have been their emotional reaction? their physical reaction? Try to think of at least six words to describe the emotions the disciples probably experienced. Write those words here.

2. Compare how you might feel in a similar, life-threatening situation. Would you find it more or less frightening than they did? Explain.

3. Jot down some dangers that threaten your physical well-being—dangers that seem unpredictable and uncontrollable.

4. Perhaps all the things you just listed could be labeled "little deaths." Threatened losses that represent for us the real thing—our own ultimate death. The Bible says that people "through fear of death [are] all their lifetime subject to bondage" (Hebrews 2:15 NKJV). How can fear keep us in bondage?

Why are we afraid? Because threats to our life and security are all around us. Calamity, loss, change, poverty, natural disasters, injury, illness—the list seems endless. Every human being experiences this kind of fear.

Fear: Source 2

We can feel afraid when other people criticize, intimidate, harass, or persecute us—justly or unjustly. It really doesn't matter. Other people often have the power to inflict emotional or physical pain on us, and we fear that.

Even "spiritual giants" have experienced this kind of fear. Take Moses, for example.

❖

One day, after Moses had grown up, he went out to where his own people were and watched them at their hard labor. He saw an Egyptian beating a Hebrew, one of his own people. Glancing this way and that and seeing no one, he killed the Egyptian and hid him in the sand. The next day he went out and saw two Hebrews fighting. He asked the one in the wrong, "Why are you hitting your fellow Hebrew?"

The man said, "Who made you ruler and judge over us? Are you thinking of killing me as you killed the Egyptian?" Then Moses was afraid and thought, "What I did must have become known."

When Pharaoh heard of this, he tried to kill Moses, but Moses fled from Pharaoh and went to live in Midian. (Exodus 2:11–15a)

1. What behavior put Moses at risk? What did he have to fear from outside forces?

2. If you are comfortable doing so, share with your partner a time when something you

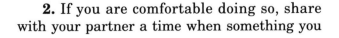

did or said got you into a "tight spot"—put you in line for criticism. Or share a situation in which you suffered unjustly from gossip, discrimination, or some form of intimidation. Was fear part of your reaction in the situations you just described? Explain that fear and the other emotions you experienced.

Why are we afraid? Because people outside us have the power to hurt us. At times our own sin brings fear-provoking consequences into our lives. At times we suffer criticism, cruelty, or rejection unjustly. Impending or actual persecution often stirs up real fear.

Fear: Source 3

We can become fearful when we look within ourselves, when we take a realistic look at the record of our lives, at many of the things we've said and done. We sometimes can't help but cringe. St. Paul said it well. Read his words from Romans 7:

❖

"I know that nothing good lives in me, that is, in my sinful nature. For I have the desire to do what is good, but I cannot carry it out. For what I do is not the good I want to do; no, the evil I do not want to do—this I keep on doing . . . . When I want to do good, evil is right there with me. For in my inner being I delight in God's law; but I see another law at work in the members of my body, waging war against the law of my mind and making me a prisoner of the law of sin at work within my members. What a wretched man I am! Who will rescue me from this body of death? Thanks be to God—through Jesus Christ our Lord!" (Romans 7:18–19, 21b–25a).

1. Can you identify with St. Paul's frustration? Explain.

2. Does your own frustration with the sin in your life ever lead to fear? Explain.

Why are we afraid? Because when we honestly look inside ourselves we see we are guilty. We know beyond doubt that we cannot please God on our own.

Fears within. Fears without. Fears all around. Who will rescue us?

Hitting Home

Fear attacks us from the inside and the outside. Fear surrounds us in this life. There's no escape. Most human beings respond to fear in different ways at different times. How do you respond to fear? Read the situations and responses from the chart on this page. Put a check beside all the responses in each column that apply to you.

When I Feel Afraid I most often. . .	When Danger Threatens Me	When Other People Threaten Me	When My Conscience Threatens Me
1. freeze up			
2. lash out (verbally or physically)			
3. run away			
4. cover up/ make excuses			
5. try to protect myself/take precautions			
6. hide/avoid			
7. cry for help			
8. laugh at it			
9. try to ignore it			
10. minimize the danger/ pretend			

1. We may respond to fear in many or even all of the ways suggested by the chart. But only one response truly opens the door to deliverance from fear. Which is it?

❖

David knew. He responded to his fear with a cry for help. His prayer begins, "I waited patiently for the LORD; He turned to me and heard my cry. . . . Be pleased, O LORD, to save me; O LORD, come quickly to help me" (Psalm 40:1, 13).

a. What things make turning to God difficult at times for many people? Take two minutes to list all that you can.

b. What things make turning to God difficult at times for you? Share, if you feel comfortable, with your partner. Remember to exercise your "pass option" if you'd rather. But in that case, jot a few notes to yourself to answer the question here:

c. How do you know how God will respond when you turn to Him?

2. Read aloud God's reassurance that He will hear our cries and quiet our fears: "Do not fear, for I am with you; do not be dismayed, for I am your God. I will strengthen you and help you; I will uphold you with my righteous right hand" (Isaiah 41:10).

3. If you feel comfortable, share with the group a time God kept that promise to you—a time He quieted your fears in a time of danger, hurt/pain, or guilt.

Wrapping Up

(Jesus said,) "I will never turn away anyone who comes to Me" (John 6:37b TEV).

Think of yourself as the "one" Jesus invites to come to Him for help in times of fear. If you respond to His invitation what can you expect from Him?

In the space below jot down one thing from this lesson you will want to remember this week to help you in times of fear:

The Extra Mile

This week read and meditate on some of the following passages. What do you hear God saying to you in these passages?

Psalm 23
Psalm 30
Proverbs 3:21–26
Isaiah 43:1–7
Hebrews 2:5–18

God, I'm Afraid— Jesus Responds to My Fear

2

Setting Our Sights

In this session we will look at how Jesus' disciples reacted in the face of fear and how Jesus responded. We will discover ways God quiets the fear we experience in our own individual lives. We will wait expectantly for His help with a current fear.

Getting Started

Imagine yourself deep in a dark, dark forest. You are moving quickly through the thick, unfamiliar territory. You cannot see the edges of the forest, nor what lies ahead or behind. You are not sure where you are going, but you keep moving as fast as you can. Your heart is pounding and your adrenalin surging. Your stomach has churned itself into a tight knot.

Suddenly, in a small clearing just ahead, a light shines. You see Jesus standing in the light. You stop. He speaks to you. What does He say?

1. Jot down your answer.

2. Share your response with a partner if you can do so comfortably. Explain why you think Jesus would speak to you this way.

Digging In

Jesus' friends and followers were average human beings, subject to the same human condition we all share. Peter, James, John, Thomas and Andrew, and all the others were real people. When they faced danger or loss, when people threatened them, when their consciences accused them, they reacted as any of us would. They felt afraid. Jesus understood this. He anticipated their reactions. He didn't just leave them alone in their misery. He came to them.

Read one of the following accounts with your partner. Then follow the directions for the exercise that follows. After a few minutes, regroup and share your insights with the entire group.

Situation 1

Jesus' disciples are about to try their wings. Jesus instructs the Twelve before He sends them on a preaching-healing mission:

❖

"I am sending you out like sheep among wolves. . . . Be on your guard against men; they will hand you over to the local councils and flog you in their synagogues. On My account you will be brought before governors and kings as witnesses to them and to the Gentiles. But when they arrest you, do not worry about what to say or how to say it. At that time you will be given what to say, for it will not be you speaking, but the Spirit of your Father speaking through you. . . . All men will hate you because of Me, but he who stands firm to the end will be saved. When you are persecuted in one place, flee to another. . . . A student is not above his teacher, nor a servant above his master. . . . So do not be afraid of them. . . . Do not be afraid of those who kill the body but cannot kill the soul. . . . Are not two sparrows sold for a penny? Yet not one of them will fall to the ground apart from the will of your Father. And even the very hairs of your head are all numbered. So don't be afraid; you are worth more than many sparrows." (Matthew 10:16–20; 22–23a; 24; 26a; 28a; 29–31)

Imagine you stood there, part of Christ's group of disciples. After you listen to your Lord you begin to talk with the other disciples. Finish each sentence with words you might hear the others saying.

1. I guess we can expect_____

_____

That's not too surprising, considering _____

_____

_____

_____

2. When I think of what's ahead, I feel

_____

because_____

_____

3. When Jesus said 'Do not be afraid,' I

_____

_____

4. I felt better when Jesus said_____

_____

_____

Situation 2

Jesus is celebrating the Passover with His disciples for the last time. During the meal He predicts His betrayal. He tells His friends He will be with them only a little longer. A sense of sadness and dread descends on them as He speaks:

Do not let your hearts be troubled. Trust in God; trust also in Me. In my Father's house are many rooms. . . . I am going there to prepare a place for you. . . . I will come back and take you to be with Me that you also may be where I am. . . . I will do whatever you ask in My name, so that the Son may bring glory to the Father. You may ask Me for anything in My name, and I will do it. . . . And I will ask the Father, and He will give you another Counselor to be with you forever—the Spirit of truth. . . . I will not leave you as orphans; I will come to you. Before long the world will not see Me anymore, but you will see Me. Because I live, you also will live. . . . He who loves Me will be loved by My Father, and I too will love Him and show myself to Him. . . . the Counselor, the Holy Spirit, whom the Father will send in

My name, will teach you all things and will remind you of everything I have said to you. Peace I leave with you; My peace I give you. I do not give to you as the world gives. Do not let your hearts be troubled and do not be afraid. (John 14:1–2a, 2c, 3b, 13–14, 16–17a, 18–19, 21b, 26–27)

Finish each sentence with words you might hear the disciples saying to one another after hearing Jesus' words.

1. When I think of Jesus leaving, my heart_____
because_____
_____.

2. I know Jesus understands how I feel because_____
_____.

3. When I heard Jesus promise to _____and _____
and _____ and _____.
and_____, I knew
_____.

4. When Jesus said, "Do not be afraid," I
_____
_____.

Situation 3

The Jewish authorities and the temple guard have come with swords and clubs to arrest Jesus in Gethsemane. They arrest Him, tie Him up, and lead Him away to trial at the house of the high priest. All the disciples run away. But Peter cautiously follows at a distance.

But when they had kindled a fire in the middle of the courtyard and had sat down together, Peter sat down with them. A servant girl saw him seated there in the firelight. She looked closely at him and said, "This man was with Him." But he denied it. "Woman, I don't know Him," he said.

A little later someone else saw him and said, "You also are one of them."

"Man, I am not!" Peter replied.

About an hour later another asserted, "Certainly this fellow was with Him, for he is a Galilean."

But Peter replied, "Man, I don't know what you're talking about!" Just as he was speaking, the rooster crowd. *The Lord turned and looked straight at Peter.* Then Peter remembered the word the Lord had spoken to him: "Before the rooster crows today, you will disown Me three times." And he went outside and wept bitterly. (Luke 22:55–62 italics added).

Imagine Peter later confiding in John. Finish each sentence with words you might have heard Peter say.

1. How could I_____

_____?

2. When that servant girl got in my face, I

_____.

3. It was _____ ,

that drove me to deny Jesus.

4. In that glance from Jesus I saw_____

_____

_____.

Situation 4

The disciples are hiding in a locked room on Easter evening. They have seen Him die in agony on the cross. Perhaps they will face a similar fate.

> On the evening of that first day of the week, when the disciples were together, with the doors locked for fear of the Jews, Jesus came and stood among them and said, "Peace be with you!" After He said this, He showed them His hands and side. The disciples were overjoyed when they saw the Lord.
>
> Again Jesus said, "Peace be with you! As the Father has sent Me, I am sending you." And with that He breathed on them and said, "Receive the Holy Spirit. If you forgive anyone his sins, they are forgiven; if you do not forgive them, they are not forgiven." (John 20:19–23)

Suppose you found yourself in the room with the disciples that night. Finish each sentence as you might have heard the disciples finish it as they talked with each other after Jesus disappeared from their sight:

1. I admit, I felt _____ cowering in that room!

2. It was reassuring when _____

_____.

3. To me, Jesus' words: Peace be with you meant _____.

4. Now I know _____

_____.

31

❖

Hitting Home

Jesus understood His disciples' fear. He anticipated it and knew how they would deal with it. Again and again He reassured them that He loved them, treasured them, had a purpose for them, would provide for them exactly what they needed. He forgave the sin their fear spawned. He replaced their anxiety with His peace.

1. Edit the paragraph in the box above so that it speaks to you personally (e.g., "Jesus [understands my] fear"). Then read the full edited paragraph aloud with your group.

Do you believe your edited version? Why?

2. Take a few minutes to reflect on your own experience. Do you ever "shake in your boots" along with Jesus' first disciples? When is this most likely to happen for you? Check all the answers that apply.

_____ When I face a particularly hard task

_____ When I face opposition and hatred for witnessing about Jesus in word or deed

_____ When I've faced major changes in my life

_____ When I face separation from a dear friend or family member

_____ When I face the possibility of my own death

_____ When I face rejection because I've let someone down

_____ When I realize I've acted like a coward

a. Tell your partner about one of those times. (Choose a time you can share comfortably, not one too personal for you or too close to your own discomfort zone.)

b. Explain how your fear affected your relationship with Christ.

c. Talk about how He helped you with your fear. How did He do that?

3. When Jesus says to us, "Do not be afraid," He is not saying "Buck up! Get a grip! Pull yourself together!" He doesn't shame us for our fear.

Neither is Jesus a disinterested clinician who observes our behavior and experience from a distance, with folded arms and furrowed brow. He, too, was human as well as divine. He understands our temptations, our pressures, our war with worry. He wants to involve Himself personally in each of our lives. He wants to teach us to trust Him. He reaches out to reassure us of His forgiving love. He promises to provide all we need to face life's dangers and uncertainties.

a. Where do you need His reassurance right now?

b. Where in the texts you read today did you hear Him speak to you about your struggles?

c. What does He promise to do to quiet your fear? How do you know?

d. How might you experience more of His peace?

Wrapping Up

Every human being experiences fear. Fear sets off within us an alarm for self-preservation. Our inborn desire to protect ourselves from danger is not a sin.

But fear does bring each of us to a crossroads. It forces us to ask, "What will I do with this fear? What are my choices? Will I panic? Will I run away? Will I freeze up or lash out? Will I give up and despair?

Or will I rely on God's mercy? Will I lean back in my Father's love? Will I relax in God's promises?

Jesus waits . . . to reassure, forgive, empower. Let Him!

The Extra Mile

This week read and meditate on some of the following passages. What do you hear God telling you about your fears and about His care for you?

John 14–17
Matthew 28
Psalm 118
Isaiah 41:10, 13
Isaiah 43:1–7

God, I'm Afraid— Love Crowds Out Fear

Setting Our Sights

In this session we will reaffirm what we know about God's deep love for us by reviewing God's action through Christ on our behalf. We will explore what it means to trust God. We will see how faith can replace fear in our individual lives.

Getting Started

Find a partner. Take turns completing the sentence below. Complete the sentence in as many ways as you can until the leader says "stop!"

Some of the sweetest words I ever heard were

What did your responses have in common with others in your group?

What conclusions can you draw based on what you discovered in this exercise?

Digging In

1. Everyone needs reassurance. How many

of your "sweetest words," in effect, reassured
you that you were:

___ accepted
___ included
___ cherished
___ restored
___ gifted (given something special)
___ reprieved
___ forgiven

2. The words we use in communicating
with others can help or hurt our relationships.
Words that reject, separate, condemn, or punish are hardly "sweet" in any ear.

Why do you think this is true?

3. Death is the ultimate separation. We all
must die someday. No one escapes unless, of
course, our Savior returns first. Scripture
clearly states the reason for this:

- There is not a righteous man on earth who
  does what is right and never sins (Ecclesi-
  astes 7:20).
- All have sinned and fall short of the glory of
  God (Romans 3:23).
- If we claim to be without sin, we deceive
  ourselves and the truth is not in us (1 John
  1:8).
- For the wages of sin is death (Romans
  6:23).
- Everyone will die for his own sin (Jeremiah
  31:30).
- The soul who sins is the one who will die
  (Ezekiel 18:4b).

❖

These words may seem bitter, hard to swallow. What feelings do these words elicit within you? Check all the responses that ring true as you reflect on your feelings. Then discuss reasons for those feelings with your partner.

_____ I want to avoid thinking or talking about death.

_____ I don't care much one way or another about death.

_____ It's inevitable, so why worry?

_____ It's hopeless. I'm doomed.

_____ I feel trapped and angry that I have to die.

_____ Death is what I deserve because I'm guilty.

_____ Sometimes I'm afraid when I think of death.

_____ Death is an experience I can't avoid.

_____ I'm terrified.

_____ I feel confident and not at all fearful.

_____ I . . .*(add your own thoughts here)*

4. Bitter words are not God's last word to us. God doesn't leave us rejected, separated, and condemned. He speaks sweet words of acceptance and reconciliation to each of us through His Son, Jesus:

37

What response do these sweet words draw out from you? Check one or more responses that reflect your feelings. Then share with your partner why you feel the way do you.

____ I feel whole and safe.

____ I'm amazed that God loves me so much!

____ I feel my anxiety melting.

____ I'm not sure these words are for me.

____ I'm wondering how God could really love me that much.

____ God is great and wonderful and generous and . . .

____ I'm touched by God's love.

____ I feel humbly thankful.

____ I . . .*(add more of your own thoughts here)*

Hitting Home

What Jesus did for us by taking our punishment and dying the death we deserved frees us from God's condemnation and assures us of eternal life. It also immediately changes our relationship with God. No longer enemies. No longer strangers or outcasts. Our Father's love draws us back into our His arms. There we are safe. We are His precious children—no longer slaves to fear, but confident of our Father's deep love for us and His power to protect us. And by our side stands our big Brother, Jesus Christ. He knows us. He accepts us. He understands us. He shares our humanness. He sacrificed Himself specifically for each one of us, stripping the devil of his power to make us his slaves by feeding our fear. Jesus, too, was tempted—yet triumphant. And so now our temptations are His concern, and He stands ready to defend us.

Who can fathom love so enormous? Yet by the power of the Holy Spirit, we trust God's love for us. That's faith. We know and believe the love that God has for us. When we trust in God's love for us, His love pushes fear out. Fear is displaced by faith.

1. Think of a time recently when fear tried to get a grip on you. (Maybe it succeeded!) Put yourself back in that situation. Now visualize the arms of God around you. Visualize God speaking softly in your ear. What would He want you to hear Him say in a time like that?

❖

Choose one or more of the passages from this lesson or other passages that help you in times of fear. You may want to look back through other lessons in this course, too. Write the passage here:

Explain to Your partner or to the members of your group why you picked the passage.

2. Being alone, cut off, can be the most fearful of human experiences. All of us need the assurance, spoken and demonstrated by a brother or sister in Christ, that God loves us and forgives us. All of us need to hear and to experience God's love in action as our fellow Christians speak God's Word to us and demonstrate His love to us.

In groups of four, form a "football huddle." Take turns praying together in the huddle. Thank God for His love. Thank Him for loving each person in your group—by name. Thank Jesus for His sacrificial death and triumphant resurrection for each of you. Ask for God's forgiveness and for the faith needed to rely on His love. Praise Him for the peace that comes from knowing His power and willingness to take care of you and to give you all you need.

Wrapping Up

Sing or speak together "How Sweet the Name of Jesus Sounds":

How sweet the name of Jesus sounds
    In a believer's ear!
It soothes our sorrows, heals our wounds,
    And drives away all fear.

It makes the wounded spirit whole
    And calms the heart's unrest;
It's manna to the hungry soul
    And to the weary, rest.

Dear name! The rock on which I build,
    My shield and hiding place;
My never-failing treasury filled
    With boundless stores of grace.

By you my prayers acceptance gain
    Although with sin defiled.
The devil charges me in vain,
    And God calls me His child.

O Jesus, shepherd, guardian, friend,
    My Prophet, Priest, and King,
My Lord, my life, my way, my end,
    Accept the praise I bring.

The Extra Mile

This week read and meditate on some of
the following passages:
Romans 8
1 John 3:19–24
Hebrews 2:9–18
1 John 4:7–21

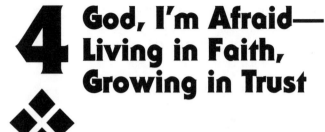

4 God, I'm Afraid— Living in Faith, Growing in Trust

Setting Our Sights

In this session we will recall God's faithfulness. We will review what it means to live in Christ. We will explore ways our trust in God can grow daily.

Getting Started

As you think about the questions that follow, try to focus on the one person you feel closest to, your closest human relationship right now. Jot down your answers. When you've finished you will share those answers you feel comfortable sharing with a partner.

1. Is there a sign/symbol of your relationship that you both recognize? What is it? What does the symbol/sign mean?

2. Think back to the beginning of your relationship with this person, perhaps to the time you first met. What specific memories do

you most treasure? What significance do you see in those early experiences?

3. How do you communicate in the context of your relationship? (E.g., notes, conversation, letters, phone calls, whispers late at night, songs.)

4. When problems arise in your relationship, how are these resolved?

5. Is there any concrete evidence of the depth of your relationship? If so, what is it?

6. Do you feel safe with this person? Why?

7. Are any other persons part of this relationship? If so, what role do they play?

❖

Digging In

We will return to these questions later. For now, return your focus to the topic of fear.

How human it is to be afraid! How we long to quiet our fears, to feel safe, to feel loved and not abandoned or rejected. How we long for close, safe relationships.

How divine it is to love, to rescue, to reassure. We've seen how Jesus has come from God to reach us, save us, and quiet our fears. God calls us now to live every day of our earthly lives in close, personal contact with Jesus, our Savior.

Don't you know that all of us who were baptized into Christ Jesus were baptized into His death? We were therefore buried with Him through baptism into death in order that, just as Christ was raised from the dead through the glory of the Father, we too may live a new life. If we have been united with Him like this in His death, we will certainly also be united with Him in His resurrection (Romans 6:3–5).

I have been crucified with Christ and I no longer live, but Christ lives in me. The life I live in the body, I live by faith in the Son of God who loved me and gave Himself for me (Galatians 2:20).

1. Read **Romans 6:3–5** and **Galatians 2:20** (above). Then think through the following questions. Share answers with your group as you feel comfortable doing so.

a. What is God saying about you—personally—in these Scripture passages?

b. What does this mean for your daily life, especially for those times you feel afraid?

c. How often do you think about your Baptism?

_____ Never

_____ When I'm in Bible class

_____ Hardly ever

_____ When someone is baptized in church

_____ Daily

_____ When my conscience bothers me

d. When you think about dying with Christ in Baptism and rising to new life, what impact does this have on your daily living?

_____ I don't fully understand what all this means.

_____ I don't think this is very important.

_____ It changes everything for me.

2. God deals with each of us personally. Think of how God called you into personal fellowship with Jesus. Think through _your_ salvation story. Jot down responses to the following questions. Then share your story with a partner.

a. How did I come to be in Christ and to have Christ living in me?

b. How did God reach me? What/whom did He use to get through to me?

c. What evidence is there in my daily life that Jesus and I are close? that I am in Christ and that Christ is in me?

45

❖

Hitting Home

1. Now let's think more deeply about our relationship with Jesus. God has drawn us into fellowship with Jesus. Through our Baptism we have died with Christ just as surely as if *we* hung on Calvary. Through our Baptism, we now live with Christ just as surely as if *we* had awakened in Joseph's garden tomb on Easter morning. We now enjoy an intimate relationship with our Lord. It's His gift to us!

God also keeps us close to Jesus, and He builds our trust in Him. Explore this a bit more by thinking through the following questions. You'll note that they are similar to the questions you answered earlier about a close human relationship. Jot down your responses.

a. What is the "sign" of your relationship with Christ?

b. When you think back to your Baptism what reassurance do you experience?

c. How do you and your Lord Jesus communicate in the context of your relationship? How often?

d. When problems arise in your relationship with Jesus—when you sin—how is this resolved?

e. What concrete evidence has Jesus provided to assure you that He gave Himself specifically for you—that He forgives you and loves you?

f. Do you feel safe in your relationship with Jesus? Explain.

g. Are any other persons part of this relationship with Jesus? If so, what part do they play?

2. Look back at your answers to the questions under "Getting Started" in which you explored a close human relationship. Then review activity 1 in this section. Keeping all this in mind, what have you discovered about the ways and means God uses to keep you in close fellowship with Jesus? Jot your thoughts down here:

❖

Wrapping Up

1. God makes it possible for us to trust Him. He gives us all we need to keep growing in trust. Where do you sense is your greatest need for growth right now?

____ Growing in repentance and confession

____ Realizing the depth of God's forgiveness

____ Feeding on God's Word

____ Recognizing my need for God's help with difficult, fear-provoking situations

____ Asking God for help instead of trying to handle things on my own

____ Recognizing God's provision and help when it comes

____ Growing in encouraging other Christians and in letting them encourage me in God's Word

2. Even though we all need to grow in all these areas, choose one of the above. Share with your partner what you will do today to let the growth begin. Then take turns praying specifically for one another that God will use His Word to build increased trust in your hearts.

The Extra Mile

This week read or meditate on some of the following passages. Copy or memorize the passages from this unit that have been most meaningful to you.

Ephesians 1:17–20
Galatians 3:26–27
Romans 13:14
Psalm 27

Helps for the Leader

1—God, I'm Afraid—Why?

❖ Getting Started

(*About 5 minutes.*) Read the session goal statement to the group ("Setting Our Sights"). Explain that this statement outlines the main points of this lesson.

Help participants find a partner. Encourage them to choose someone other than a close friend or family member. Ask them to follow the directions for this introductory activity.

❖ Digging In

Read the opening paragraph to the group. Each of the Scripture passages in this section reveals a different direction from which fear can attack us.

Fear: Source 1. (*About 8 minutes.*) Encourage participants to read the text from Matthew 8 and to jot down their answers for 1–4. Then share comments.

Make sure everyone understands that the instinct for self-preservation is not sinful. But also point out the possibility that at times we exaggerate or even imagine dangers that aren't really there.

Focus especially on question 4. Much of what we fear can be traced back to personal loss—of a job, of financial security, of health, of a relationship, and, ultimately, of our life itself.

Read the last paragraph in this section aloud.

Fear: Source 2. (*About 8 minutes.*) Have participants read through this section on their own and then discuss 1 and 2 with one another. If they have trouble with question 2, be prepared to share an example from your own life.

Then read the last paragraph in this section aloud.

Encourage group members to underline words or phrases that help them catch the main points in each section.

Fear: Source 3. (*About 8 minutes.*) Encourage everyone to be as honest as possible with themselves and one another. Before discussing the questions in 1 and 2, you may want to ask a volunteer to read the passage from Romans aloud. As you finish this section read the last two paragraphs to the group. Emphasize again that not all fear comes from sin, but some of it does. And although physical threats to life and limb from storms, floods, and other natural phenomenon must be taken seriously, and although other people have the capacity to hurt us deeply, the gravest threat to us comes from unforgiven sin. We remain in grave danger until sin is forgiven and the fear it brings is allayed.

❖ Hitting Home

Have a volunteer read the opening paragraph in this section. Allow participants about three minutes to complete the chart. Then ask if some members of the group are willing to share what they learned about themselves through this activity.

1. (*1 minute.*) Number 7 on the chart ("Cry for help"), in particular, crying to God for help in Christ, opens the door to deliverance from fear. Ask a volunteer to read David's words from **Ps. 40:1.**

a. Work together as a group to do this.

b. Encourage participants to think this through on their own. If possible, they should share their thoughts with a partner. But emphasize the pass option and invite anyone who wants to work alone to do that without any penalty from the group.

c. We know our Lord will hear and help because of Jesus and His cross. This question is the pivotal question of this session. Don't pass over it lightly. As the apostle Paul points out in **Romans 8,** our heavenly Father did not hold back His own, dearly loved Son; He gave Him up to death on the cross—all for us. We need not fear that He is holding a fistful of IOU's with which to accuse us and for which He intends to punish us. He has completely forgiven us for Jesus' sake.

When we experience the fears of a guilty conscience, we can come to God, confess our sin, and receive His assurance of complete pardon and the assurance of the righteousness (right standing with God) that is now ours in Christ.

Since God has indeed helped us with our biggest, most frightening problem—our sin and the judgment we deserved because of it, we can also trust Him to help us with our other problems and fears too—no matter how overwhelming they may be. Include pride, self-sufficiency, and unbelief in your list among the other things participants mention.

2. (*2 minutes.*) Read the verse from **Isaiah 41** aloud, perhaps asking the group to read it in unison. Allow time for the words to sink in. Then read the following paragraphs aloud to the group:

Your God loves you uniquely. Not in general, but specifically. He loves you specifically. He is deeply concerned about you as a particular person. You are worth infinite value because He paid an infinite price for you. He loves you constantly and consistently, even when you sin!

Your God's heart overflows with mercy and compassion for you. Nothing you can do could ever make Him stop loving you. He knows your fears. He is patient with those fears. When you are frozen with fear or running away from Him, or pretending to be brave, you can stop. You can stop running. You can let Him lift you up in His mighty arms and hold you tight against His heart. He wants to do that for you. He wants it very much! (**Cf. Luke 12:24; Jer. 31:3; Ps. 63:3; James 5:11; Rom. 8:39; John 10:11; and Is. 40:11.**)

3. (*2 minutes.*) Ask volunteers to share their personal stories of a time God quieted their fears. God speaks to us through His Word. God works through His Word. Listen for ways God's Word has quieted fears in the stories that are told.

❖ Wrapping Up

Have everyone read **John 6:37** aloud. Allow about three minutes for each person to complete the activity in this section. If time permits, ask volunteers to share one thing from this lesson he/she will remember this week in dealing with fear.

❖ The Extra Mile

Before participants leave, spend some time in group prayer. (Check the suggestions at the front of this guide.)

The passages referenced in this section could form the foundation for participants' devotional reading during the coming week. Suggest that as they read they jot down what they hear God telling them about their fears and about ways He wants to help them in their fears.

2—God, I'm Afraid—Jesus Responds to My Fear

❖ Getting Started

(*About 2 minutes.*) Read aloud the goal statement for the lesson ("**Setting Our Sights**"). Then move directly into the opening activity. To do this, help everyone link up with a partner.

This exercise may be a new kind of activity for many in the group. Its purpose is not to suggest that our Lord will reveal Himself outside His Word or that everyone in the group who's spiritually healthy will have a personal experience like the one described. God speaks to us today in Holy Scripture. He comes to us in His Word and in the Sacraments.

The activity should help participants see, however, what they expect God's response to their fears will be. The dramatic, imaginary confrontation should jar loose fears, especially the unhelpful kind of fear, even Christians sometimes have of God and the mistrust we carry in our hearts because of our sin.

On the other hand, those who respond to the imaginary scenario with relief that help has come, can thank their Lord for the faith-creating work His Spirit has done in their hearts.

❖ Digging In

(*About 5 minutes in groups of 2 or 3, then 20 minutes for whole group discussion.*) Read aloud the opening paragraph. Note that Jesus' friends reacted to fear as humanly as we do. Explain that they will read four accounts from Scripture that show this. More important, the accounts show us how Jesus responded to His friends' fears, how He helped them with it.

Ask the group to divide the four accounts among themselves—each set of partners working on a different account at the same time. If you have a large group, let participants work in groups of three or four.

After the small groups have had a chance to study their account and complete the sentences, call for the attention of the whole group. Allow volunteers from each group to summarize the account they read and to share ways group members completed the sentences. Encourage participants to explain why they answered as they did. If time is short, focus particularly on the accounts from **Luke 22** and **John 20**.

It may be helpful to note the following:

Situation 1

The disciples would face great physical danger (hatred, arrest, flogging, persecution). Their fear of this might quite naturally cause them to back away or avoid their mission. Their fear might lead them to doubt God's ability to protect

54
❖

them or to doubt God's wisdom in allowing such persecution.

But Jesus tells them clearly what to expect. *He* is sending them. *He* is equipping them. *He* is using them to witness for Him. The Spirit will work powerfully through them. They are loved, valued, treasured. Jesus has anticipated that they might be worried or upset or fearful, and He has reassured them that they can trust His provision for them.

Situation 2

The disciples face a great loss—Jesus, their teacher and best friend, is going to leave them. Surely they must feel grieved, confused, abandoned, rejected. Their fear of abandonment may lead to depression. The thought of facing an uncertain future could immobilize them. Such fear might cause them to doubt that any good could come of Jesus' leaving. Such fear might cause them to doubt God's love for them.

But Jesus urges them to trust Him. He tells them clearly what He plans to do: prepare for them, return for them, grant their requests, provide the mighty Counselor, who will stay forever and teach them. He soothes their troubled hearts with His own perfect peace. Jesus understands how they feel, and He has provided perfectly for them.

Situation 3

Peter faces the danger of arrest and possible death because of his friendship with Jesus. Peter's in-born instinct for self-preservation is not sin. This kind of fear serves as an alarm that triggers Peter's instinct to live. But the fear leads Peter to doubt God. (Here is a perfect example of fear spawning sin.) As Peter begins to doubt God's ability to protect him, the disciple tries to protect himself. Thus he denies the Lord, cursing and swearing.

But Jesus' confrontation—His penetrating glance—breaks the cycle. Jesus' kindness leads Peter to repentance and brings him God's forgiveness. (See **Rom. 2:4.**) Jesus further responds to Peter's shame with His mercy.

Situation 4

The disciples fear the religious authorities. They face the danger of arrest and possible death. Perhaps they also fear Jesus' rejection, for they have abandoned Him, run away when He needed them most. Their fears might cause them to doubt God's willingness to forgive or to protect them. That road of doubt dead-ends at shame and despair.

But Jesus comes to them! Not to condemn them, but to bring them peace. He reassures the disciples, Peter among them, that He has accepted and forgiven them and that He values them and wants to send them into His service. He gives them the Holy Spirit that they might also share the Good News of forgiveness with others. Jesus takes the initiative. He does not allow their fear to separate them from Him or to deflect them from the mission He has chosen for them!

❖ Hitting Home

1. (*About 4 minutes.*) This paragraph summarizes Jesus' response to His disciples' fears. Ask a volunteer to read it aloud. Then as a group edit the paragraph so it speaks to the reader personally. Ask participants to delete and insert words as necessary. Then ask the group to read aloud the edited version.

Let participants comment on whether they find it hard to believe the edited version. What makes us reluctant to trust God's care for us?

2. (*About 5 minutes.*) Invite individuals to identify with Jesus' disciples. Encourage everyone to work alone on the check list and then to think about how they would respond to **a, b,** and **c** before sharing with their partner. Encourage everyone to offer an incident they can share with comfort, one that's not too threatening or too recent.

3. (*About 7 minutes.*) Read the two opening paragraphs with the whole group. Then encourage partners to share their answers to *a–d*. As the discussion winds down, comment briefly on *c* and *d*. Remind the group once again that we can know He will keep His promise to strengthen and help because we've stood beneath the cross to see Jesus Christ die there for us. His Word assures us in no uncertain terms of His love, and our Savior sealed those assurances for us with His own blood. As we open our hearts to His Word, as we listen to that Word spoken in the weekly worship service, as we remember His Word spoken over us in our Baptism, claiming us as His own, as we receive His Word of promise and forgiveness in the Lord's Supper ("given and shed for you"), as we let God soften and then saturate our hearts with His Word of promise, we experience more and more of His peace.

❖ Wrapping Up

(*About 2 minutes.*) Read this material aloud together thoughtfully and slowly. Then close with prayer. Pray specifically for those needs that have been shared with the group.

❖ The Extra Mile

Point out the passages referenced in the last section of this lesson. Suggest that the readings become part of everyone's devotional life during the coming week. Perhaps participants could copy those words and phrases from the readings that have special meaning for them and share these next time as you get started.

3—God, I'm Afraid—Love Crowds Out Fear

❖ Getting Started

(*About 3 minutes.*) Read aloud the goal statement for this session ("Setting Our Sights"). Then give participants a few moments to find a partner. Be sensitive to individual needs and personalities in your group. Be sure everyone feels comfortable and included.

Ask the partners to work together to create a list as directed in the study guide section. After two minutes, ask if anyone wishes to share conclusions with the whole group. Some possible sentence completions might include:

"I love you"; "I forgive you"; "Welcome"; "I'm glad you're my mom!"

❖❖ Digging In

1. (*About 2 minutes.*) Allow time for individual reflection. Then ask a volunteer or two to share an example of how their "sweetest words" made them feel accepted, included, or cherished.

2. (*About 2 minutes.*) Read these paragraphs aloud to the group. Ask for volunteers to answer.

Note that before the Fall, Adam and Eve lived in perfect fellowship with one another and with God. There was no separation, no brokenness. God designed human hearts to live in unity, in community, in fellowship. Sin opened a great gulf between God and sinners. It created a chasm between human beings, too. It's not surprising, then, that psychologists tell us that fear of rejection is universal in human hearts. We long for the sweet words of acceptance and reconciliation; yet we fear the opposite. That fear itself can widen the rifts that divide us from one another and from our Lord.

3. (*About 6 minutes.*) Read the first paragraph aloud to the group. In order for everyone to hear and realize the full impact of these words of Law, take turns reading each passage aloud. Challenge readers to read expressively, like a righteous judge. These are not sweet words. They should be read accordingly. Give each member a chance to read at least one passage. Read the passages more than one time, if necessary.

Next, give everyone a chance to complete the checklist and to discuss their response with a partner. Participants who opt to write their own personal response may do so in the blank space.

58

4. *(About 6 minutes.)* Follow a procedure similar to that in activity 3. Everyone should see this as an opportunity to hear and realize the impact of the Gospel in all its sweetness. Again, challenge readers to read the passages expressively, as they would a letter from a loving friend or parent.

Once again give everyone a chance to complete the checklist and to share their response with a partner. Those individuals who choose to write their own response may do so in the space provided.

❖ Hitting Home

(About 6 minutes.) Ask an effective reader to read the first two paragraphs slowly and meaningfully. Then reread the second paragraph yourself. Ask volunteers to tell what these words mean to them.

Encourage candor. It's not always easy to trust God's love—not because God's love is weak—but because Satan continually whispers doubt: "You're not good enough, loving enough, faithful enough. All you've done wrong has ruined any chance of your ever being reconciled to God. You've blown it so many times, God has given up on you. Something awful is going to happen to you."

The Word of God counters Satan's lies! Over and over God reassures us that He loves us, that He loves us unconditionally! The Scripture cradles Christ, God's Son and our Savior. The words of Scripture reassure us that the final word of God is a word of perfect love. When we trust that Word, then all the things that scare us—illness, injury, divorce, rejection, loss, change, our sins, even death itself—lose their threat. Like water flushing out a bottle, His love fills us up and replaces our fear.

1. *(About 4 minutes.)* Allow everyone to reflect as they complete the next part of the exercise. Then ask everyone to share the words of Scripture that help them in times of fear.

2. *(About 15 minutes.)* Ask an effective reader to read the first paragraph. Then ask volunteers to tell what these words mean to them.

59
❖

Next read the directions for the "football huddle." Explain that the groups may pray for one another using the prayer suggestions listed in the exercise. Encourage individuals to offer prayers that are personal and relevant to those in each group. Don't hurry this time. Allow this experience to demonstrate God's love for each person.

Encourage those who feel comfortable to put their arms around one another's shoulders to actually form a huddle as they pray. This will help keep the mood light and may alleviate part of the shyness some may feel at praying aloud. The physical contact can also help people express their Christian affection and concern for one another in a nonthreatening way. If some feel uncomfortable with this, it's okay. Simply ask them to sit close to one another as they pray.

❖ Wrapping Up

(*About 2 minutes.*) As the prayer groups finish, ask participants to turn to the hymn. Speak or sing through the verses worshipfully.

Explain that the hymn was written by John Newton who also wrote "Amazing Grace." Newton wrote so powerfully about the grace of God because he had experienced it so personally and abundantly. A seaman at an early age, he described himself in his autobiography as a young man whose principles were totally corrupted—out of control—"exceedingly vile indeed." He admitted: "I not only sinned with a high hand myself, but made it my study to tempt and seduce others upon every occasion."

Yet this slave trader was changed by God's grace and became an ordained minister and hymn writer: "Let me not fail to praise that grace which could pardon, that blood which could expiate, such sins as mine. . . . I, who was the willing slave of every evil, possessed with a legion of unclean spirits, have been spared and saved, and changed to stand as a monument of His almighty power forever." (*John Newton: An Autobiography*)

60

❖ The Extra Mile

Ask for volunteers, if anyone wishes, to share any words or phrases from last week's readings that they found especially meaningful. Remind everyone that we all need constant reassurance from God's Word. Reading and meditating on God's Word each day allows His love to crowd out our fears. Ask for ideas from the group on how to use the suggested readings at home during the week.

4—God, I'm Afraid—Living in Faith, Growing in Trust

❖ Getting Started

(*About 10 minutes.*) Read the goal statement to the group ("Setting Our Sights"). Then move directly into the introductory exercise. Ask participants to follow the directions. Suggest they jot down words or phrases as they think through answers to the questions on pages 40–41, but point out there is no need to write out lengthy answers. Allow about four minutes for individual work. Call time and suggest each partner take about three minutes to share what he/she feels comfortable sharing. You will return to this exercise at the end of the session. Its significance will become apparent at that point.

❖ Digging In

Read aloud the introductory paragraphs and the passages from Romans and Galatians.

1. (*About 8 minutes.*) Allow about three minutes for individuals to reflect on the two Scripture passages and to complete the questions and checklists in *a–d*. Then spend about five minutes in whole group discussion. If people have trouble getting started, read the following aloud:

In Baptism God ties us so tightly to Jesus Christ that we die with Him and we rise with Him. We live a new life now—right now. We live in Christ. He lives His life in and through us.

In your discussion, focus on *b* and *d*. Help participants see the connection between what God has done in connecting them so intimately with Christ's death and resurrection and their individual daily lives right now. Because Christ is in us and we are in Him, we need not fear. The guilt of our sins, the evil in our world, the power of the devil—nothing ultimately can hurt us. What Christ has done for us by claiming us as His own and what He has done in us by wrapping us in His own death and resurrection in our Baptism, gives us inexhaustible confidence!

We can trust that He has our best interests at heart. Because He has overcome sin and death for us, we can rely on His power and willingness to protect us and to provide for us in every circumstance. While not all our earthly experiences will be what we might wish and while some of them may be in fact tragic and even horrible, our Lord will see us through them. He will allow nothing to crush us. He will use His Word to strengthen us in our troubles, and He will mold and shape us through our difficulties to make us more like Jesus (Rom. 8:28) What a fantastic promise!

2. *(About 10 minutes.)* Read the opening paragraph to the group. Allow three minutes for individual reflection. Then call time and ask partners to take turns sharing their own salvation stories. If participants are having trouble with *c* encourage them to come back to it after completing "Hitting Home."

❖ Hitting Home

1. *(About 10 minutes.)* Read the opening paragraph aloud. A key sentence is *God also keeps us close to Jesus, and*

He builds our trust in Him. You may want to ask everyone to underline this sentence.

As group members work through the answers to *a–g* they will probably notice similarities to the opening exercise in which they analyzed a significant human relationship. They should also note the specific ways God builds our trust in Christ through His Word—the Holy Scriptures, the Word connected with the visible elements of Baptism and the Lord's Supper, and the Word we hear from the pulpit and from one another as we encourage one another in Jesus.

You may want to sum up this section by reading aloud the following:

"God, who has called you into fellowship with His Son Jesus Christ our Lord, is faithful" (1 Cor. 1:9). Every day our faithful God calls us to repentance and confession. And every day we claim the forgiveness He promises us: "When you were dead in your sins . . . God made you alive with Christ. He forgave us all our sins" (Col. 2:13).

Every day our faithful God is ready to speak to us in His Word. "For everything that was written in the past was written to teach us, so that through endurance and the encouragement of the Scriptures we might have hope" (Romans 15:4).

Daily God listens to us in our prayers and praise. He reminds us, "Don't worry about anything, but pray about everything. With thankful hearts offer up your prayers and requests to God. Then, because you belong to Christ Jesus, God will bless you with peace that no one can completely understand. And this peace will control the way you think and feel" (Philippians 4:6–7 CEV).

Regularly God offers us the personal assurance that Jesus is in us, with us, and for us: "This is my body given for you, . . . This cup is the new covenant in my blood, which is poured out for you." (Luke 22:19, 20).

And if all that were not enough, our faithful God surrounds us with "little Christs" who, also baptized into Him, help us and hold us much like He does. "Your life in Christ makes you strong, and His love comforts

you. You have fellowship with the Spirit, and you have kindness and compassion for one another" (Philippians 2:1 TEV).

If we ignore or neglect any of these gifts God uses to strengthen our trust in Him we leave ourselves open to fear. As we embrace His gifts, our trust grows steadily stronger.

An option: Copy the Bible passages included in the paragraphs above. Distribute the sheet to group members ahead of time and assign each passage to a specific participant. Read the summary section aloud, asking participants to read the passage you assigned them at the appropriate point.

2. *(About 1 minute.)* Ask everyone to read the directions and write their conclusions. Ask if anyone wishes to share what he/she has written.

❖ Wrapping Up

1. *(About 2 minutes.)* Allow time for individuals to respond. They may check more than one item. Tell them no one will have to share their responses.

2. *(About 4 minutes.)* Read the directions to the group. Allow time for partners to talk and pray together. Urge them to share only what they feel confortable sharing.

As you close, suggest that partners and/or group members keep in touch with one another to encourage each other. Offer to talk with anyone who feels afraid in the days ahead. Remind the group that fighting fear and growing in trust is an ongoing process.

❖ The Extra Mile

Encourage everyone to use the references listed here in their daily devotions this week.